Medieval Warfare

JAYN ARNOLD • GLEN DOWNEY

Editorial Board
David Booth • Joan Green • Jack Booth

STECK-VAUGHN
Harcourt Achieve

www.HarcourtAchieve.com

10801 N. Mopac Expressway
Building # 3
Austin, TX 78759
1.800.531.5015

Steck-Vaughn is a trademark of Harcourt Achieve Inc. registered in the
United States of America and/or other jurisdictions. All inquiries should
be mailed to Harcourt Achieve Inc., P.O. Box 27010, Austin, TX 78755.

Ru'bicon © 2006 Rubicon Publishing Inc.
www.rubiconpublishing.com

Project Editors: Miriam Bardswich, Kim Koh
Editor: Kermin Bhot
Creative Director: Jennifer Drew-Tremblay
Art Director: Jen Harvey
Designer: Gabriela Castillo

6 7 8 9 10   5 4 3 2 1

Medieval Warfare
ISBN 1-4190-2454-X

CONTENTS

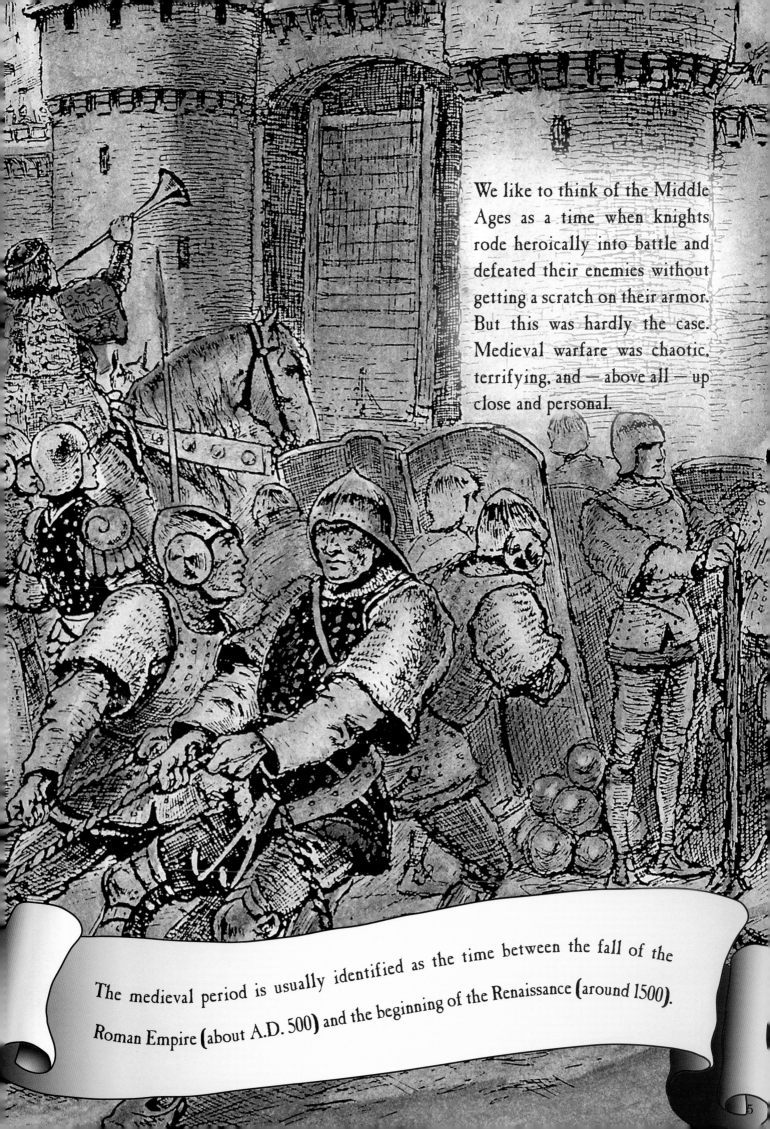

We like to think of the Middle Ages as a time when knights rode heroically into battle and defeated their enemies without getting a scratch on their armor. But this was hardly the case. Medieval warfare was chaotic, terrifying, and — above all — up close and personal.

The medieval period is usually identified as the time between the fall of the Roman Empire (about A.D. 500) and the beginning of the Renaissance (around 1500).

ARMED AND DANGEROUS

warm up

In a small group, discuss movies and TV programs you have seen about medieval warfare. What weapons were most commonly used?

Many fearsome weapons were used on the medieval battlefield. Although they might appear to be simple by today's standards, these weapons could, in the hands of experienced soldiers, destroy vast enemy armies. Here are some of the most popular medieval weapons.

THE CROSSBOW

The crossbow consists of a prod (which is like a bow) fastened to a stock that contains a trigger. Once the string of the bow is pulled into place and the quarrel is inserted, the weapon is ready to fire. The crossbow replaced the longbow. It took longer to load and fire, but it could be mastered quickly and could be used to fire large quarrels at an enemy. The crossbow was likely invented in China but was used throughout Europe in the Middle Ages.

quarrel: *a short, heavy, square-headed arrow or bolt*

THE PIKE

The pike was a huge pole with a sharpened metal tip used in medieval Europe to unseat cavalry and protect those with short-range weapons. Sometimes exceeding 20 feet in length, pikes could inflict serious damage on the battlefield.

CURVED SWORDS

The Katana: a curved, single-edged sword used by Samurai warriors in medieval Japan.

The Kilij: a Turkish curved sword that could wreak havoc against an opponent.

Other curved swords were the Indian tulwar and the Persian shamshir. The curved blade allowed the sword to cut with great power and cause fatal wounds with less effort.

wreak havoc: *cause devastating damage*

THE MACE, MORNINGSTAR, AND FLAIL

The mace was a weapon with a heavy blunt object stuck at the end of a pole. It was a popular weapon in medieval Europe because it could knock an opponent down or knock him off his horse. When the head of the mace was substituted with a ball and spikes, it was known as a morningstar. When a length of chain separated the head from the pole, the weapon was known as a flail. All three were deadly weapons in combat.

BREAKING AND ENTERING: A SIEGE

The castle was the heart of medieval defense. Defenders could fire arrows at advancing enemies or pour flaming oil on them to prevent a successful breach of the fortress.

breach: *break-through*

Imagine preparing to attack a castle.

As the invading army, you would make sure that your **ballistae** are in good working order. These oversized crossbows could fire one or more giant bolts a great distance, terrorizing those perched on the castle's battlements.

While your ballistae are aimed at the defenders, your **catapults** will be firing large boulders capable of damaging the castle walls and crushing your enemies. You'll strike fear into the hearts of your opponents when they see these missiles in flight!

And, of course, your **trebuchets** will need to be active as well. They can only fire a missile or two an hour, but they make clever use of a counter-weight device to fire huge boulders like a giant sling!

Catapult

Trebuchet

Storming of Castle from a 15th century French manuscript.

While the enemy is occupied, you have the perfect opportunity of sending in your **siege towers**. These large-wheeled structures house soldiers who are ready to leap onto the castle walls!

Hopefully, your enemies will be so occupied that they won't see you running siege ladders up to the castle walls. These ladders are great for getting your soldiers up and over the castle walls as you get your last siege weapon into place.

Now all you need to do is bring down the main gate with giant **battering rams**! These can be simple logs either carried by several men or mounted on wheels and rocked back and forth in order to strike the gate repeatedly. Once the gate comes crashing down, your infantry pours in and the castle's defenders surrender!

FYI

Another technique for getting into a castle was called "sapping." An attacking army would dig tunnels underneath an opponent's castle, fill them with flammable liquid, and then ignite them. This would cause an explosion and destroy the castle's foundation.

wrap up

1. From the descriptions, choose the siege weapon that you think would be the most effective. List the reasons for your choice.

2. Imagine you are the lord of a castle under siege. Describe your reactions to the attack.

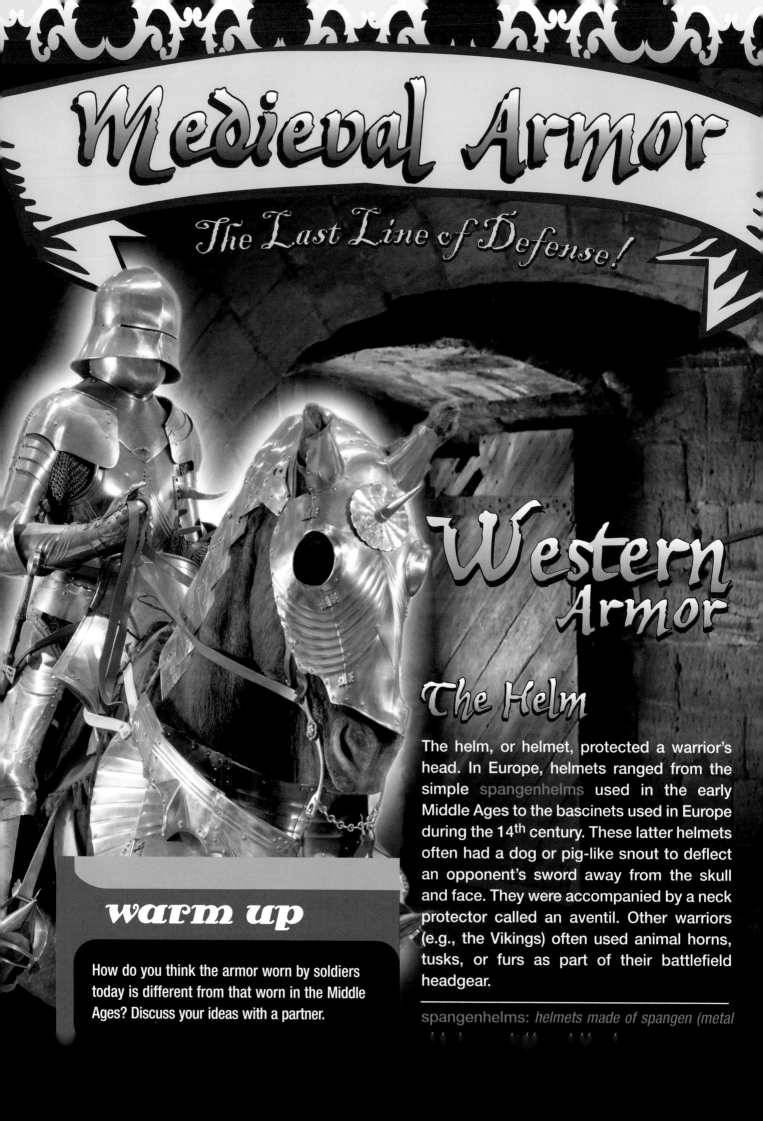

Medieval Armor

The Last Line of Defense!

Western Armor

The Helm

The helm, or helmet, protected a warrior's head. In Europe, helmets ranged from the simple spangenhelms used in the early Middle Ages to the bascinets used in Europe during the 14th century. These latter helmets often had a dog or pig-like snout to deflect an opponent's sword away from the skull and face. They were accompanied by a neck protector called an aventil. Other warriors (e.g., the Vikings) often used animal horns, tusks, or furs as part of their battlefield headgear.

spangenhelms: *helmets made of spangen (metal*

warm up

How do you think the armor worn by soldiers today is different from that worn in the Middle Ages? Discuss your ideas with a partner.

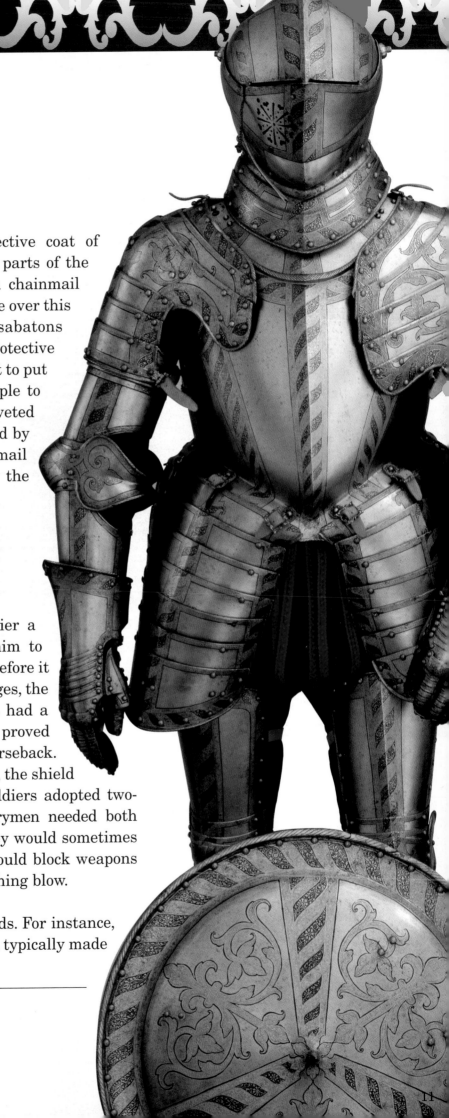

The Armor

It made for a cumbersome but effective coat of protection, covering the most exposed parts of the body. Often the knight would wear a chainmail coat of interlocking iron rings, and place over this a breastplate, gauntlets, greaves, sabatons (metal shoes or boots), and other protective gear. It was a tiring process for a knight to put on his armor, and he usually had people to help him. Plate mail (plates of metal riveted together) replaced chainmail. First used by the ancient Greeks and Romans, plate mail was adopted by medieval knights in the 13th century.

The Shield

A shield was a way of giving a soldier a second line of defense by allowing him to block an unfriendly blow or projectile before it got to the armor. In the early Middle Ages, the kite shield was popular in Europe. It had a rounded top and pointed bottom, and it proved useful for a knight mounted on horseback. During the later Middle Ages, however, the shield became rarer on the battlefield as soldiers adopted two-handed weapons. Soldiers and infantrymen needed both hands for their weapons. However, they would sometimes use a buckler, a smaller shield that could block weapons but also strike the enemy with a punching blow.

Different warriors used different shields. For instance, the Vikings were fond of round shields, typically made of wood.

cumbersome: *bulky and heavy*
greaves: *armor for the shin*

Middle Eastern Armor

Arabic Warrior

During the Crusades, Europeans often ran into lightly armored but fast-moving Muslim opponents. Although Middle Eastern armor varied from one area to another, it was generally lighter than that worn by Europeans. Muslim warriors, for example, typically wore the mail coat (or hauberk) rather than full plate armor.

Sometimes Muslim warriors wore armor consisting of rectangular plates (called lamellar armor) fashioned onto a leather coat — a combination which proved quite effective. They often carried a round shield used in combination with an ax or saber. These differences made sense given their warmer climate and the general strategies they employed on the battlefield, such as using a bow and arrow while on horseback.

Advantage of Light Armor

For Muslim warriors, the speed that light armor gave them on the battlefield was essential. Because they were able to strike and retreat, or surround an enemy quickly, Middle Eastern armies often had the initial advantage over their opponents. In 1102, when the Christian king of Jerusalem, Baldwin the First, confronted the Egyptian army in the Second Battle of Ramleh, he was expecting a very small enemy force. When he came over a rise and saw that the Muslim army was huge, he was unable to retreat because the fast-moving Egyptians were already beginning to surround him. He was forced to attack head-on, with disastrous results.

rise: *spot higher than surrounding ground*

wrap up

1. Create a chart listing the various pieces of Western and Middle Eastern armor. Beside each piece write its use.

2. With a partner, design your own set of medieval armor, label it, and share it with the class.

WEB CONNECTIONS

Research online for more information about medieval armor. Share your findings with the class.

The Battle

Have you ever shown sportsmanship, only to have an opponent get the better of you because of it? Have you ever seen this happen to someone else? Share your experiences with a partner.

The year was 991. Viking pirates were raiding the coast of England, demanding payment from the nobles if they wanted the attacks to end. The English king, Aethelred II (appropriately known as Aethelred the Unready) had little choice but to raise taxes in order to pay off the Viking invaders.

One of these invasions was led by Olaf Tryggvason (trU-gva-sOn), a Norwegian warrior, whose band of a few thousand men was set to land near the River Blackwater in Essex. Byrhtnoth, an English commander, led a small band of men to meet the Vikings as they came ashore. He might have been able to resist the Viking attack if it had not been for his tragic act of chivalry.

Instead of slaying the Vikings as they waded through the low tide from a nearby island to shore, Byrhtnoth allowed them to land in order to have a fair fight. This, however, was a mistake, since he and his men were outnumbered and overpowered. Byrhtnoth was slain, and the English ranks were thrown into chaos, with many soldiers fleeing in panic.

---

chivalry: *medieval code of behavior, including honor, fairness, and courage*

CHECKPOINT

Do you agree with Byrhtnoth's decision to allow the Vikings to cross at low tide without attacking them right away?

# of Maldon

Viking invasion led by Olaf Tryggvason

Byrhtnoth's "thegns," his personal circle of men, decided to sacrifice themselves by fighting to the death in order to avenge the death of their leader.

In the following excerpt from the Anglo-Saxon poem *The Battle of Maldon*, they are inspired by Byrhtwald, a longtime supporter.

The Battle of Maldon

Translated by Mary K. Savelli

Byrhtwald spoke, lifting up his shield;

he was an old companion, shaking his ash spear.

He very boldly advised the warriors:

"Thought must be the stronger, heart the bolder,

courage must be the greater,

as our strength lessens.

Here lies our elder all hewed,

the good man, on sand. A kinsman thinks

to lament who now turns from war-play.

I am old of life; from here I will not go,

but I think to lie myself down

beside my lord, by so dear a man."

---

hewed: *hacked or cut*
lament: *mourn*

wrap up

1. With a partner, discuss how Byrhtwald's speech might have inspired his fellow warriors to continue fighting.

2. Using some of the words from the poem, write a short speech to inspire a soldier heading into war today. Read your speech to the class.

Thought must be the stronger, heart the bolder, courage must be the greater, as our strength lessens.

WEB CONNECTIONS

Search the Internet to find more information about Byrhtnoth, Olaf Tryggvason, or the Battle of Maldon itself. Choose a site that you think is particularly good and prepare a short presentation on it to the class.

FIGHTING FACTS

warm up

In a small group, brainstorm unusual facts you know about war. You may wish to share information you learned from books or movies.

The Hundred Years War (1337–1453) between England and France did not actually last 100 years — it lasted 116!

If you attended Oxford University during the Middle Ages, there was a policy forbidding you from bringing your bow and arrows to class.

The Mongol warriors from eastern Asia knew how to demoralize an enemy. On the first night of a siege, the Mongol leader would use a white tent. This meant that if the castle surrendered, all lives would be spared. On the second night, his tent was red. This meant that only the women and children would be spared. On the third night, he emerged from a black tent — no one would be spared.

According to "The Peace of God," issued by the Roman Catholic Church in the 11th century, certain people and property could not be harmed during conflict. It was intended to protect those who could not defend themselves, including children, women, clergy — and farm animals! It also prohibited nobles from invading churches, beating the defenseless, burning houses, and committing other such acts.

According to "The Truce of God," Thursday through Sunday were declared days of peace. In addition, there could be no violence during certain religious festivals and throughout Lent.

demoralize: *destroy the confidence of*
prohibited: *did not permit*

Medieval armies sometimes used their catapults to fire dead bodies into the enemy's castle. It was hoped that the insects feeding on the corpses would spread disease among those living in the castle.

The most important military invention of the Middle Ages was not an elaborate weapon or suit of armor. It was the stirrup. This allowed cavalrymen to fight while on horseback, and completely changed the way battles were fought.

catapults: *machines used to throw things over a great distance*

wrap up

Choose one of the facts that you find interesting, and explain why to a partner.

WEB CONNECTIONS

Use the Internet to find three more interesting facts about medieval warfare that could be added to the ones found here. Share these with your classmates.

Dangerous Waters

Kublai Khan's fleet sailing in the Indian Ocean, by William Blake

20

War on the High Seas

Naval warfare in the Middle Ages emphasized the capture of enemy ships. Deliberately sinking enemy ships was seen as a terrible waste. Instead, the idea was to ram an enemy ship or get close enough to board it, then capture the crew and take the ship as a prize.

Before the 14th century, galleys, which were low, flat vessels, rowed by slaves, were used on the high seas. These were replaced by sailing ships that could maneuver better and be built higher. Higher ships gave the advantage to the attacker using flaming arrows and missiles.

Sailors sometimes threw lime and other dangerous chemicals at enemy ships. At other times they threw soapy water at their opponents' deck in order to make their enemies slip and fall.

missiles: *weapons that are thrown*
lime: *a chemical that burns when combined with water*

The Naval Conquests That Never Were

Kublai Khan (1215 – 1294), grandson of Genghis Khan, was a great Mongol leader. He successfully invaded China using a large fleet of ships and brilliant military strategy to defeat the Song dynasty. However, once he had secured China and moved the capital of his empire to Beijing, his Mongol compatriots pressured him to undertake further expansion. He decided to conquer Japan.

> ## CHECKPOINT
> As you read, check out how Kublai Khan was really defeated.

In 1274, his large naval invasion force quickly made its way from island to island until it was met by an enemy that no fleet of ships ever wants to encounter — a storm. The fleet had to retreat, despite having the firepower to have defeated the Japanese.

compatriots: *fellow citizens*

If this setback was not bad enough, Kublai Khan decided to invade Japan again in 1281. This time his fleet of more than 100,000 Chinese and Mongol soldiers ran into both Japanese resistance and something far more deadly — a hurricane! Kublai Khan's ships were thrown into chaos. Some sank, others were captured, and nearly half of the fleet retreated. The Japanese were so amazed by their good fortune that they called the storms *kamikaze*, meaning divine winds.

This could not have sat well with Kublai Khan. He tried to invade elsewhere, and selected the island of Java off the coast of Indonesia. This time his ships sailed with confidence into calmer waters and began the invasion. But something much smaller and far more harmful than a hurricane lay in wait for them — disease. Those who managed to avoid sickness and death were forced to retreat, and Kublai Khan's naval invasions were once again unsuccessful.

Old Rivals at Sea

The first victory for the English in the Hundred Years War was the Battle of Sluys on June 24, 1340. In this massive naval battle, the English forces, led by King Edward III, managed to defeat a superior number of French ships by using rather sophisticated tactics. Because the French had tied their ships together to create a tight defensive position, a common strategy in the Middle Ages, Edward had his own fleet maneuver so that the sun was behind them.

Some accounts argue that this tactic made the French believe Edward was fleeing and they untied their boats to pursue, only to have the English immediately turn to engage them in ship-to-ship fighting. Although the French were great in number, Edward and his men overwhelmed them, capturing and destroying many of the ships in the French fleet. The victory was a resounding success for Edward III, and it marked the beginning of a great military career.

wrap up

Create a naval recruitment poster that could have been used to enlist sailors to join either Kublai Khan's or Edward III's fleet.

WEB CONNECTIONS

With a partner, use the Internet to find information on either Kublai Khan or Edward III. Write a character sketch using your information.

FREEDOM!

warm up

Discuss with a partner the qualities that you would look for in a war hero.

Robert the Bruce fighting an English knight, during the Battle of Bannockburn

24

It was June 23, 1314. The Scots, led by their king, Robert the Bruce, were preparing to meet the English at the Battle of Bannockburn. Robert rallied his troops, recalling the bravery of Scottish hero William Wallace.

Wallace had become a legendary hero to the Scots in 1297, after he and Andrew de Moray had overcome the much larger English force at Stirling Bridge. Andrew de Moray died of his wounds, but Scottish casualties were limited, and Wallace was later knighted by Robert the Bruce.

The following year Wallace met the English in the Battle of Falkirk. Once again, the Scots were outnumbered. This time Wallace was defeated and later charged with treason by the English, dragged through the streets, hanged, and drawn and quartered.

---

drawn and quartered: *organs are removed and burned while the person is still alive. Then the torso is cut into four parts.*

Robert the Bruce's passionate words to his troops at Bannockburn are remembered in Robert (Robbie) Burns' poem *Scots Wha Hae* ("Scots Who Have").

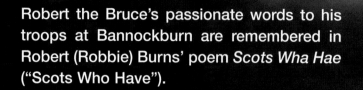

Scots Wha Hae

By Robert Burns

Scots, **wha hae wi**' Wallace bled,   who have with
Scots, **wham** Bruce has **aften** led;   whom, often
Welcome to your gory bed,
    Or to victory!

Now's the day, and now's the hour;
See the front o' battle **lour**;   tower
See approach proud Edward's power —
    Chains and slavery!

Wha will be a traitor knave?
Wha can fill a coward's grave!
Wha sae base as be a slave?   who's so
    Let him turn and flee!

Wha for Scotland's king and law
Freedom's sword will strongly draw,
Freeman stand, or freeman **fa'**,   fall
    Let him follow me!

By oppression's woes and pains!
By your sons in servile chains!
We will drain our dearest veins,
    But they shall be free!

Lay the proud usurpers low!
Tyrants fall in every foe!
Liberty's in every blow! —
    Let us do or die!

servile: *-slave-like*
usurpers: *those who seize another's authority or rights*

At Bannockburn the Scots defeated the much larger English army under King Edward II. The battle established Scottish independence although war with England was not officially over for another 14 years. Scottish independence would not be lost until after the death of Queen Elizabeth I (1603) when King James VI of Scotland became James I of England.

Robert the Bruce is still generally regarded as Scotland's greatest hero, known both for his "courage and humanity."

In 1995, Mel Gibson directed and starred in *Braveheart*, a film loosely based on the life of William Wallace. Many of the events described in the film, including the murders of Scots at the beginning, never took place. Most significant is the film's misrepresentation of Robert the Bruce as an opportunist, almost a traitor. Robert the Bruce was actually working with Wallace when the Battle of Falkirk took place. This was likely 50 miles away at Ayr, where he destroyed the castle to prevent the English from using it as a base. Robert the Bruce and his father had no connection with the capture of Wallace.

opportunist: *someone who takes advantage of a situation for his or her own benefit*

wrap up

1. With a partner, read Robbie Burns' poem aloud, alternating stanzas.

2. Write a tribute to Robert the Bruce or to William Wallace. Use the Internet or the library to find additional information.

Women of WAR

Illustrations by Colin Mayne

warm up

What do you think the primary roles, responsibilities, and occupations of women were during the Middle Ages? Discuss your opinions with a partner.

The battlefields of the Middle Ages were dominated by men. Nevertheless, there were a number of women who showed political and military expertise that often proved more than a match for their male counterparts. As you read, pay attention to the personality characteristics that the following women have in common.

counterparts: *people who have similar functions and characteristics*

Matilda, Countess of Tuscany

(1046–1115)

Matilda of Tuscany — sometimes called Matilda of Canossa — was an Italian countess. While she was still a child, Matilda had to deal with the murder of her father, the deaths of her brother and sister, and the knowledge that she would inherit vast amounts of land. As an adult, Matilda's military accomplishments helped to protect her country from the forces of King Henry IV of Germany. Matilda and Henry IV disagreed over who the rightful Pope of the Roman Catholic Church should be. This debate was called the Investiture Controversy. It is still highly debated by historians today.

Matilda decisively defeated Henry IV's forces at Sobara in July, 1084, although his forces later drove her into the mountains. Matilda defeated Henry again in October, 1092.

Hangaku Gozen

(late 12th century – early 13th century)

Hangaku Gozen, a young woman from a family of warriors in north central Japan, was legendary for her strength and accuracy with a bow. In 1201, she and her fellow warriors were defending Tossaka Castle from enemy forces when she positioned herself on the roof of a nearby storehouse. She did so despite making herself a target of numerous warriors armed with spears and arrows. She was eventually wounded in both legs, captured, and taken prisoner. In some versions of the story, Hangaku eventually married and lived happily ever after, but in other versions she was killed in a later battle.

Jeanne d'Arc

Jeanne d'Arc

(1412 – 1431)

Jeanne d'Arc, or Joan of Arc, was only a teenager when she helped lead the French army to victory at the Battle of Orleans during the Hundred Years War. Inspired by voices of angels and saints, she convinced King Charles VII of France to oppose the English advances. In a bold move, the king gave her a white suit of armor and command over the French troops despite the fact that she had no military training. At Orleans she had a vision that the French should attack from the north. They did so, entering the besieged city on April 29, 1429.

Over the next year, Jeanne led the French in reclaiming several fortifications and an important bridge, forcing the English to retreat.

Jeanne was captured by the Burgundians and sold to the English in 1430. The English turned her over to a church court in France to be tried for heresy and witchcraft. She was found guilty after months in prison, and then burned at the stake. She was later found innocent of all charges, and in 1920 was declared a saint by the Roman Catholic Church.

heresy: *beliefs that go against those of an established religion*

CHECKPOINT

The Duke of Burgundy was a rival for the French throne.

wrap up

1. Which of the women depicted here has, in your opinion, the most impressive accomplishments? Prepare notes for an informal class discussion in which you defend your choice.

2. Which illustration do you think most effectively captures the spirit of the woman it depicts? List three reasons to support your choice.

Illustrated by JEREMY BENNISON

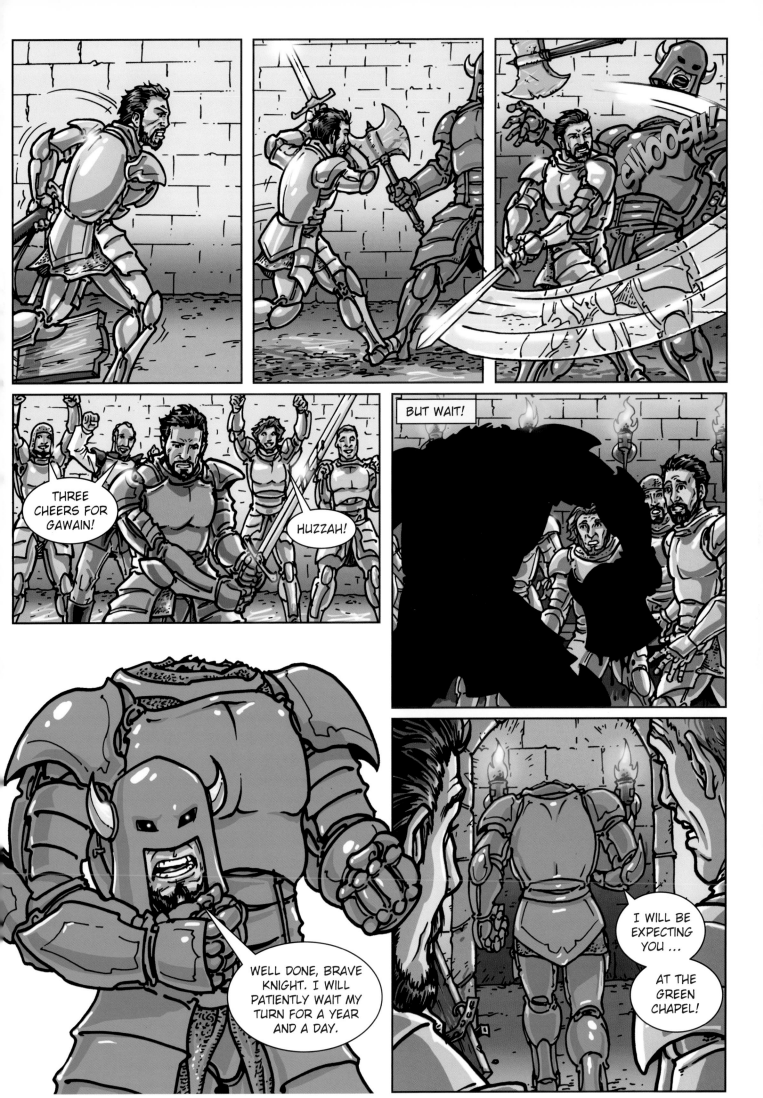

THE YEAR IS ALMOST OVER AND SIR GAWAIN PREPARES FOR HIS JOURNEY.

SOB

TAKE HEART, GOOD FRIENDS. I WILL BE BACK SOON.

HE TRAVELS FOR MANY WEEKS, OVERCOMING OBSTACLES AND DEFEATING ENEMIES ALONG THE WAY.

BAM!

UNTIL ONE DAY ...

I SHALL REST HERE AND GATHER STRENGTH FOR THE FINAL STAGE OF MY JOURNEY.

ONCE INSIDE, HE IS GREETED BY THE LORD OF THE CASTLE.

WELCOME GOOD SIR! YOU MAY REST YOUR TIRED BONES HERE.

PROVIDED THAT AT THE END OF EACH DAY WE EXCHANGE WHATEVER WE HAVE ACQUIRED.

A FAIR BARGAIN.

... BUT WHAT'S THE CATCH?

EACH DAY THE EXCHANGE TAKES PLACE.

ON THE FINAL DAY, THE LADY OF THE CASTLE COMES TO VISIT.

I SENSE YOU MUST SOON CONFRONT A GREAT FOE.

THIS MAGICAL CLOAK WILL PROTECT YOU FROM HARM.

The Death of a King:
The Battle
of Bosworth Field

warm up

Should kings, presidents, and other world leaders fight alongside the soldiers that they send off to war? Discuss this with a partner.

The scene is Bosworth Field on August 22, 1485. Richard III, King of England, is trying desperately to hold on to his kingdom while Henry Tudor, Second Earl of Richmond, is trying to defeat the king and claim the throne.

England had suffered constant fighting during the previous 30 years because of the conflict between Richard's family (the House of York) and Henry (who had ties to the House of Lancaster). This war was known as the War of the Roses, named for the white rose that symbolized the House of York, and the red rose that symbolized the House of Lancaster.

Henry Tudor receiving the crown of King Richard III at the Battle of Bosworth Field.

During the 16th century, William Shakespeare wrote a play about King Richard III. Elizabeth I, ruler of England at the time, was the granddaughter of Henry Tudor. Richard, Henry's enemy, is depicted in the play as a cruel, murderous, hunchbacked villain who will stop at nothing to achieve and maintain power.

Near the end of the play, Richard must face Henry Tudor's forces on the battlefield. Throughout the battle, Richard defeats many opponents. On five occasions he thinks he has killed Henry Tudor himself. Finally, near the end, Richard is unseated from his horse and must fight on foot. In this excerpt from Shakespeare's *Richard III*, we see Richard, along with his supporters Sir William Catesby and the Duke of Norfolk, in the final moments before his death.

Act V, Scene iv. Another part of the field.

Alarum: Enter Norfolk and Forces Fighting

CATESBY
Rescue, my Lord of Norfolk, rescue, rescue!
The king enacts more wonders than a man,
Daring an opposite to every danger:
His horse is slain, and all on foot he fights,
Seeking for Richmond in the throat of death.
Rescue, fair lord, or else the day is lost!

Alarums. Enter King Richard III

KING RICHARD III
A horse! a horse! my kingdom for a horse!

CATESBY
Withdraw, my lord; I'll help you to a horse.

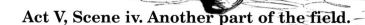

Alarum: *military sounds*
Withdraw: *leave the scene of the fighting*

KING RICHARD III

Slave, I have set my life upon a cast,
And I will stand the hazard of the die:
I think there be six Richmonds in the field;
Five have I slain to-day instead of him.
A horse! a horse! my kingdom for a horse!

Exeunt

CHECKPOINT

What suggests that Richard III is very upset with what is happening on the battlefield?

The scene ends and so does the reign of Richard III. He is betrayed by two of his supporters who, unknown to Richard, have also agreed to fight on the side of Henry Tudor. When they see Henry's forces have the upper hand, they surround and kill Richard. Their treachery brings the battle to a swift and decisive end. It is said that Richard's body was then dragged naked through the streets.

The War of the Roses was now essentially over, and with it, medieval warfare in England. So many nobles had been killed over the previous 30 years that there were few left to oppose Henry Tudor, now Henry VII, the new King of England.

FYI

It was not unusual to use decoys in battles — soldiers dressed up like a king or general. The decoys were meant to draw enemy fire away from the real king or general. (See Richard's comment about killing five Richmonds in the battlefield.)

---

cast: *throw of a die*
Exeunt: *Latin for end of scene; everyone exits*

wrap up

1. You are a war correspondent at the scene of this battle. Write a short report of the battle for your newspaper.

2. Imagine that it is the eve of the Battle of Bosworth Field and you, as King Richard III, are trying to boost the morale of your troops. Write a speech that would inspire them to fight with courage and honor.

WEB CONNECTIONS

Use the Internet to find differences between the historic Richard III and Shakespeare's portrayal of him. Share your findings with the class.

SUNDIATA:
HERO OF THE MALI EMPIRE

warm up

Why do you think our knowledge of African medieval history might not be as complete as our knowledge of what happened in Europe during this time?

FYI

The present-day Republic of Mali is a nation of 12.3 million people located southwest of Algeria. It is among the poorest countries in the world, with 65% of its land area being either desert or semi-desert.

While European empires were being built and destroyed, three great empires rose and fell in the heart of western Africa. These empires, Ghana, Mali, and Songhay, dominated the African landscape and changed the course of the continent's history. The story of the Mali Empire is especially fascinating because it was founded in the 13th century by a famous warrior named Sundiata Keita. He overcame a frightening enemy to lay the foundation for one of the greatest empires in history. In the following poem, Sundiata is wondering about the battle he must fight against Sumanguru, King of the Sosso people.

You ask me if I am afraid.

When I was born I could not walk. I was
(ignored)
misunderstood

"The little lame boy of the Mandinkan king,"
they sneered.
"He'll never rule."

They might be right.

If Sumanguru defeats me today,
If I fall to him at Kirina
No songs will they sing of Sundiata
No griots tell of my struggle
How I learned to walk with a staff of iron
How I learned to run from persecution
How I learned to stand and fight.

And now as I ride into battle
My worst enemy confronts me.
Not Sumanguru, though he is powerful,

but myself.

Can I honor the memory of a father?
Overcome a dangerous foe?
Forge a new empire?

I don't know.

But what I do know is more important.
For Sumanguru's sacred animal is the rooster,
And I have tipped my finest arrow with its spur.

I am the lost son who has returned,
I am the lame child who can walk,
I am the king without his crown,
I am, and am not, many things.

You ask me if I am afraid.

We will see.

griots: *oral historians*
spur: *a growth on the foot or wing of some birds*

wrap up

List the adjectives found in the poem to
describe Sundiata and Sumanguru. With a
partner, brainstorm additional adjectives to
describe each one.

WEB CONNECTIONS

Use the Internet to find information on
the Ghana, Mali, or Songhay empire.
Prepare a brief presentation for the class.

Safe Passage From Jerusalem

warm up

Have you ever questioned someone's behavior only to realize that you didn't fully understand it at first? How did you feel?

*T*he Crusades were wars waged by Christian Europe to regain Palestine (the Holy Land) from Muslim control. In A.D. 660, Arab Muslims had conquered Palestine but had allowed Christian pilgrims to visit. However, when Seljuk Turks invaded Palestine in 1078, they started persecuting Christians. Soon they were threatening the city of Constantinople. The emperor of Constantinople was a Christian and, fearing invasion, he asked the pope for help. In 1095, Pope Urban II called for all Christians to start a holy war against the Seljuk Turks and reclaim the Holy Land.

Between 1095 and 1187, there were three Crusades. In the following story, Muslim forces under Saladin have just conquered the Holy City of Jerusalem.

It's 1187, and Saladin's forces have just conquered the city of Jerusalem. As the Muslim commander prepares to escort the Christians out of the city, one of his officers has serious doubts about his leader's military strategy.

HAMZA'S CONFUSION

"I don't get it."

Hamza was still confused after his audience with Saladin, general of the Muslim forces. He was ordered to give safe passage from Jerusalem to thousands of defeated Christians. Now, back at his tent, he found himself shaking his head.

"How will we ever put an end to this nonsense if we allow our enemies time to recover their strength?" He respected Saladin and would carry out his orders but he still didn't understand why they would allow the Christians safe passage.

As he left his tent and gave instructions to the men accompanying him on the journey, Hamza continued to wonder at Saladin's capacity for generosity. Perhaps he had just been outwitted by Balian, the leader of the

↑

CHECKPOINT
Why do you think Saladin agreed to the lesser amount?

LEAVING JERUSALEM

Christian forces. Saladin had asked for 100,000 bezants to free all of the captives but had been bargained down to a mere 30,000!

Hamza looked up to see three large processions of Christians beginning to make their way out of the city. The Templars were leading the first column and the Hospitallers the second. Balian and Heraclius, Patriarch of Jerusalem, headed the third.

His lieutenant and good friend, Kateb, had finished assembling the troops and was now standing with him.

FYI
The Knights Templar and the Hospitallers were Christian military religious groups. They were set up to protect pilgrims traveling in the Holy Land.

"We could have had many more slaves," Hamza mumbled, his eyes fixed on the swelling columns.

bezants: *gold coins of the Roman empire used in Europe during the Middle Ages*
Patriarch: *Bishop*

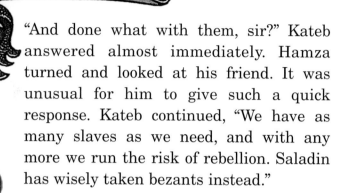

"And done what with them, sir?" Kateb answered almost immediately. Hamza turned and looked at his friend. It was unusual for him to give such a quick response. Kateb continued, "We have as many slaves as we need, and with any more we run the risk of rebellion. Saladin has wisely taken bezants instead."

Hamza had not thought of this. With so many Christians leaving Jerusalem, Saladin would not have to worry about those sold into captivity. He could use his revenues to build his army and avoid insurrections while he attacked elsewhere.

CHECKPOINT
Reflect on the two advantages arising from Saladin's decision.

"We are to follow at a distance, ensure the Christians' safe passage, and see where fate takes them. Have the men follow my lead, Kateb."

"It shall be done."

The three columns of Christian refugees had now filed out of Jerusalem and were making their way across the open countryside. Hamza ordered his men to keep a respectable distance and to avoid harassing

insurrections: *rebellions*

any of their defeated foes. "They have paid their ransom," he said to his men as they set out, "and they have earned their freedom."

HAMZA'S DOUBTS CONTINUE

But did he really believe what he was telling them? "Why do we allow them safe passage? Are we simply to permit them to heal themselves and invade again when they have recovered?" Hamza could not understand it, even as he was carrying out the general's wishes. "Perhaps there is wisdom in some of his generosity, but certainly not in this." And Hamza was once again bewildered as he led his troops behind the three columns. He was ordered to follow them for three days and then return to the holy city, so that is what he would do.

CHECKPOINT
Can you visualize this?

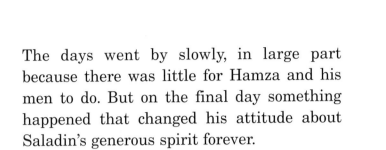

The days went by slowly, in large part because there was little for Hamza and his men to do. But on the final day something happened that changed his attitude about Saladin's generous spirit forever.

As the Christians began making their camp for the evening, Hamza paid careful attention to what they did and realized that the Christians followed the same course of action every evening. They erected their tents, said their prayers, and posted guards to protect the perimeter. This was vital information about how the Christians set up their camps and defended them. No wonder Saladin had sent him and his men to follow the Christian exodus from the city. It was very clever military strategy!

Hamza smiled to himself. He would have much to tell Saladin on his return, and much to thank him for.

"Now I get it."

---

exodus: *departure of a large group of people at the same time*

wrap up

1. Reread the story. Create a flow chart of the events in the story. Include the main questions that Hamza asks himself.

2. With a partner, role-play a scene between Saladin and Hamza upon Hamza's return to Jerusalem.

WEB CONNECTIONS

Search the Internet to find more information about the Medieval Crusades. Then create a timeline of the major battles fought during the Crusades.

ACKNOWLEDGMENTS

The publisher gratefully acknowledges the following for permission to reprint copyrighted material in this book.

Every reasonable effort has been made to trace the owners of copyrighted material and to make due acknowledgment. Any errors or omissions drawn to our attention will be gladly rectified in future editions.

Robert Burns: "Scots Wha Hae." Courtesy of Representative Poetry Online (2005), the University of Toronto.

Mary K. Savelli: "The Battle of Maldon." Permission courtesy of Mary K. Savelli.